The POETRY of
SNOWDONIA

The POETRY of
SNOWDONIA

Edited by Tony Curtis

SEREN BOOKS
*1989

SEREN BOOKS is the book imprint of
Poetry Wales Press Ltd.,
Andmar House, Tondu Road,
Bridgend, Mid Glamorgan

Selection and Introduction
© Tony Curtis, 1989

The Acknowledgements page is an extension of the
copyright statement

ISBN 1-85411-008-X

Cover painting: 'Waterfall Cwm Glas' by Kyffin Williams
Cover design by Jeane Rees

*The publisher acknowledges the financial support of the
Welsh Arts Council*

Typeset in 10½ point Plantin by Megaron, Cardiff
Printed by The Camelot Press plc, Southampton

CONTENTS

The Lakes

The Coastline

Introduction

This anthology is the first of its kind. It represents an up to date selection of the best poetry in English and Welsh written in or about north Wales. There are familiar poems and famous poets here for some of the finest poetry in English has been written in this region. I have also made available translations of poems from the Welsh language by R. Williams Parry, Gwyn Thomas, Euros Bowen and others, for north Wales has inspired writers in at least two languages. Indeed this region with Snowdonia at its heart has held a special significance for artists and writers since Giraldus Cambrensis — Gerald of Wales — made his great journey around Wales in 1188. He wrote:

> I must not fail to tell you about the mountains which are called Eryri by the Welsh and by the English Snowdon, that is the Snow Mountains. They rise gradually from the land of the sons of Cynan and extend northwards near Degannwy. When looked at from Anglesey, they seem to rear their lofty summits right up to the clouds. They are thought to be so enormous and to extend so far that, as the old saying goes, 'Just as Anglesey can supply all the inhabitants of Wales with corn, so, if all the herds were gathered together, Snowdon could afford sufficient pasture'.
> — *The Journey Through Wales*, translated by Lewis Thorpe.

There is a poetic tradition which predates even that. The princes of Wales were generous in their patronage of bards who worked for their masters as politicians and historians in verse and I have included a poem by Hywel ab Owain Gwynedd written even earlier in the twelfth century, "I love today what the English hate, the open land of the North". The longstanding independence of the people of north Wales and the pressures brought to subdue them are recreated in modern poems by John Tripp, Gillian Clarke, R.S. Thomas and others.

The eighteenth century in a sense re-discovered the natural poetry of this landscape as the Romantic sensibility was drawn to the beauty of Snowdonia. William Wordsworth, Shelley and

Robert Southey are represented in these pages. They, and the other visitors who came after them, were, of course, seeing what they wanted to see. There is an imagination which creatively alters landscape and life as it perceives places and people. Certainly, the priest Gerard Manley Hopkins, at the end of the nineteenth century, responded to his time in Clwyd by producing some of the most astounding poetry in English literature, poems which rise above the place and beyond time.

A hundred years later another priest, the Anglican R.S. Thomas, is forging a body of work in north Wales which is as fine as any in the world. In an example of the contentious issue of langauge in Gwynedd, however, Thomas has declined to have any of his poems included in this anthology, preferring to call Snowdonia by its Welsh name, Eryri. North Wales has in recent years been subject to other economic and political pressures of peculiar force. The poets of Wales have responded to those pressures with poems quickened by fire and urgency. *The Poetry of Snowdonia* could not be simply a nature anthology; this book represents north Wales, its landscape and its communities, as it really is — beautiful, bilingual, angry, witty, thoughtful, threatened, resilient. I have made a selection which will, I trust, intrigue and provoke you. This is a book which contributes to the experience of north Wales both for visitors who "Spend here your measure of time and treasure" and those who, with T.H. Parry-Williams, can say "There are bits of me scattered all over that land".

Tony Curtis

The Mountains

ON LEAVING LONDON FOR WALES

Hail to thee, Cambria, for the unfettered wind
   Which from thy wilds even now methinks I feel
Chasing the clouds that roll in wrath behind
   And tightening the soul's laxest nerves to steel!
True! Mountain Liberty alone may heal
   The pain which Custom's obduracies bring,
And he who dares in fancy even to steal
   One draught from Snowdon's ever-sacred spring
Blots out the unholiest rede of worldly witnessing.

And shall that soul to selfish peace resigned
   So soon forget the woe its fellows share?
Can Snowdon's Lethe from the freeborn mind
   So soon the page of injured penury tear?
Does this fine mass of human passion dare
   To sleep, unhonouring the patriot's fall,
Or life's sweet load in quietude to bear
   While millions famish even in Luxury's hall
And Tyranny high-raised stern lowers over all?

No, Cambria! never may thy matchless vales
   A heart so false to hope and virtue shield,
Nor ever may thy spirit-breathing gales
   Waft freshness to the slaves who dare to yield.
For me! . . . the weapon that I burn to wield
   I seek amid thy rocks to ruin hurled
That Reason's flag may over Freedom's field,
   Symbol of bloodless victory, wave unfurled —
A meteor-sign of love effulgent o'er the world . . .

Do thou, wild Cambria, calm each struggling thought;
   Cast thy sweet veil of rocks and woods between,
That by the soul to indignation wrought
   Mountains and dells be mingled with the scene.
Let me forever be what I have been,

But not forever at my needy door
Let Misery linger, speechless, pale and lean.
  I am the friend of the unfriended poor;
Let me not madly stain their righteous cause in gore.

Percy Bysshe Shelley

GUARD'S VAN TO WALES

Via Euston, via the Friday rush,
  Via starting-time arrears
I landed in the guard's van with
  A scree of mountaineers.

All corduroyed and confident
  They cluttered up the floor
With rucksacks, ropes and one-man tents
  And climbing-gear galore.

Sprawled careless on the oil-soaked boards
  Basic to all guard's vans
They spread their multi-coloured maps
  Discussing craggy plans.

And I, still dressed in City rig,
  Nostalgic and *de trop*,
Eavesdropped along the rocky routes
  I'd scrambled long ago,

As, bumping through the gusty dark
  We followed mountain trails
With foothold and belaying point
  From Euston up to Wales.

By Ogwen and her guardian heights
  Their talking carried me
To Idwal's nail-scarred slabs and past
  The cauldron of Twll Du.

Till Bangor's gloomy station yard,
  Gale-swept and slatey-wet,
Reminded me what different ways
  Our compasses were set.

Robert Chaloner

15

CLIMBING CADER IDRIS

(for a mountaineer)

You know the mountain with your body,
I with my mind, I suppose.
Each, in our way, describes
the steepening angle of rock.

What difference now as we,
falling into step and conversation,
put to the test our long
thigh muscles and our breath,

turning together to the open view,
a distant plough, a lozenge of field.
We face the slope again, our boots
rough-riding the scree up, up . . .

. . . past the last ruined hafod, the last flower,
stream falling among boulders,
the mountain ewe and her lamb and at last
Llyn Cau like a secret cupped in hands.

You climb on to the summit
'to test my body further'.
I prefer to stare at shirred water
and the vast face of stone.

I search for words.
While I'm still catching my breath
you describe that dizzy joy
at the sheer page,

'A move so delicate
along a traverse,
just fingertip
between the hold and the fall'.

Gillian Clarke

CRÎB GOCH

Shout —
you will not disturb the flock on these slopes,
the waterfall of stone sheep,
the unhurried, unbleating panic,
the headlong, motionless rush:
that mountains of ice have shepherded,
that ice and snow and mist have clothed,
that wind and storm have sheared
in the green youth of the world, —
you cannot frighten these.

Shout — throw your rope
(unless the wind snatches your thread-thin voice)
a thousand hanging feet
about the horns of the bull-dusk whose terrible butting
stands between you and daylight.

Shout —
words are not current here:
were they not born yesterday,
were they not baby-mouthed
in a cave over there?

T. Rowland Hughes

(Translated by R. Gerallt Jones)

CADWALLA'S LONELY HUT

That lonely dwelling stood among the hills,
By a grey mountain-stream; just elevate
Above the winter torrents did it stand,
Upon a craggy bank; an orchard slope
Arose behind, and joyous was the scene,
In early summer, when those antic trees
Shone with their blushing blossoms, and the flax
Twinkled beneath the breeze its liveliest green.
But, save the flax-field and that orchard slope,
All else was desolate, and now all wore
One sober hue; the narrow vale which wound
Among the hills, was grey with rocks, that peered
Above its shallow soil; the mountain side
Was loose with stones bestrewn, which, oftentimes
Sliding beneath the foot of straggling goat,
Clattered adown the steep, or huger crags,
Which, when the coming frost should loosen them,
Would thunder down. All things assorted well
With that grey mountain hue; the low stone lines,
Which scarcely seemed to be the work of man,
The dwelling, rudely reared with stones unhewn,
The stubble flax, the crooked apple-trees,
Grey with their fleecy moss and misseltoe,
The white-barked birch, now leafless, and the ash,
Whose knotted roots were like the rifted rock
Thro' which they forced their way. Adown the vale,
Broken by stones, and o'er a stoney bed,
Rolled the loud mountain-stream.

Robert Southey

CLIMBING SNOWDON

(from *The Prelude*, 1805)

In one of these excursions, travelling then
Through Wales on foot, and with a youthful Friend,
I left Bethkelet's huts at couching-time,
And westward took my way to see the sun
Rise from the top of Snowdon. Having reach'd
The Cottage at the Mountain's Foot, we there
Rouz'd up the Shepherd, who by ancient right
Of office is the Stranger's usual guide;
And after short refreshment sallied forth.

   It was a Summer's night, a close warm night,
Wan, dull and glaring, with a dripping mist
Low-hung and thick that cover'd all the sky,
Half threatening storm and rain; but on we went
Uncheck'd, being full of heart and having faith
In our tried Pilot. Little could we see
Hemm'd round on every side with fog and damp,
And, after ordinary travellers' chat
With our Conductor, silently we sank
Each into commerce with his private thoughts:
Thus did we breast the ascent, and by myself
Was nothing either seen or heard the while
Which took me from my musings, save that once
The Shepherd's Cur did to his own great joy
Unearth a hedgehog in the mountain crags
Round which he made a barking turbulent.
This small adventure, for even such it seemed
In that wild place and at the dead of night,
Being over and forgotten, on we wound
In silence as before. With forehead bent
Earthward, as if in opposition set
Against an enemy, I panted up
With eager pace, and no less eager thoughts.
Thus might we wear perhaps an hour away,

Ascending at loose distance each from each,
And I, as chanced, the foremost of the Band;
When at my feet the ground appear'd to brighten,
And with a step or two seem'd brighter still;
Nor had I time to ask the cause of this,
For instantly a Light upon the turf
Fell like a flash: I looked about, and lo!
The Moon stood naked in the Heavens, at height
Immense above my head, and on the shore
I found myself of a huge sea of mist,
Which, meek and silent, rested at my feet:
A hundred hills their dusky backs upheaved
All over this still Ocean, and beyond,
Far, far beyond, the vapours shot themselves,
In headlands, tongues, and promontory shapes,
Into the Sea, the real Sea, that seem'd
To dwindle, and give up its majesty,
Usurp'd upon as far as sight could reach.
Meanwhile, the Moon look'd down upon this shew
In single glory, and we stood, the mist
Touching our very feet; and from the shore
At distance not the third part of a mile
Was a blue chasm; a fracture in the vapour,
A deep and gloomy breathing-place through which
Mounted the roar of waters, torrents, streams
Innumerable, roaring with one voice.
The universal spectacle throughout
Was shaped for admiration and delight,
Grand in itself alone, but in that breach
Through which the homeless voice of waters rose,
That dark deep thoroughfare had Nature lodg'd
The Soul, the Imagination of the whole.

William Wordsworth

SNOWDON 1798

No doubt you find it hard to credit, the rude
rock dropping behind in a smother of mist,
that the air, holding you with its stillness, plots
river, plain and wood with such exactitude;
so wide a prospect, the earth curving beneath
your eye from far inland smoke to western sea.
The difference is not the climbing, the steep ascent
successfully concluded, conquest of scree and heath,
but the exultation of inward music,
such as a hawk might hear, threading time and space
with omniscient eye as he rides the high wind's
combers when its curling surf breasts the walled rock.

Already, far below, the last shreds of day
dissolve in rising night: here the thin air
questions your unexpected dream, the wonder
which usurped an urban sensibility;
and as you descend, feeling the crumbling stone
slip beneath your feet, already shaping words
for comfort, you tell yourself that no one
sees the light who does not know our common dark.

John Stuart Williams

CONVICTION

I stood, like a god, just at the corner where
The old Red Trail near mighty Snowdon's summit
Turns left, a level rock-strewn path, and there,
Like one who can rule fate, boldly, and straight
Down the tangled cliff, I rolled a massive stone,
And I watched it swiftly gallop, with a group
Of small rocks in a racing competition,
As it set them going clattering down the slope.
I knew full well that it was I alone
— The god, indeed — who gave this role to play
To the foolish stone, and fashioned the design
Of each move since I sent it on its way.
But then I realized, when it was gone,
I was no god — what I was was the stone.

T.H. Parry-Williams

(Translated by Joseph P. Clancy)

SHE'LL BE COMING ROUND THE MOUNTAIN

Space and time entangle in this
patchy world, almost at the top
of Wales, where blurred shades scramble
the horizons and winds fire
thorns into my face. Droplets
coalesce on the cold window pane
of my forehead, trickle
into my mouth. This wild womb
has taken me in and I exult
as the wind makes a drum of my hood.

The thorns have turned to arrows fired
from longbows in the valley
and their song rises to the pitch
of ice on glass. The streams become
a torrent and my tongue chills under
its flow. Your little girl is too fragile
for this mountain and you will have
turned. I open my hood to the wind
and rest on a green-skinned block of granite.

Strange, as I sit here, staring at my
boots against the scudding cloud, how the
wind plays tricks. Fragments of the human
voice flit by, cohere, and are
shuffled by my mind into an old
song. Then, like the Cheshire cat, a smile
congeals in the mist, linked loosely
to a pair of tennis shoes, light-footing, a slim
hand clasping a smaller one, jerkily swinging.

John Latham

WELSH INN PARLOUR

Keep that old gramophone going.
For heaven's sake don't let's just sit and think.
Talk? Why, whatever should we talk about?
We know what everybody's been doing.
Let's have a good time. Let's have a drink.
Let's hear the band play, hear the boys shout.
Let's have some noise to kick the blue devils out.
Keep the old gramophone going.

And half a mile away
There's silence on the hills and the stars' slow dance.
It's cold out there. But one might sit and think
With a great-coat on. One might even kneel and pray.
At any rate one could give one's soul a chance,
And the world wouldn't have to shrink
To a blur of noise and drink
This way.

There, the world's firm shape,
It's true and lasting shape not to be denied,
Background of all the ages that make man's day,
Stands to the dark as a cape
To sea, juts chinlike into the cosmic tide.
There, you could see the universe wheel and obey
Laws that your children learn at their schools. And you play
The gramophone, to escape.

Will you not escape from escaping? See, the moon
Comes and the stars draw back. For such as me
Your Welsh hills and your bright skies are spread out.
Break those scratched records, smash that bastard croon.
The world's whole past and all futurity
Are waiting on the mountainside. The rout
Of heaven do homage to you. Their soundless shout
Drowns out the loud empty tune.

Geoffrey Faber

WE HAVE NO NEED TO DREAM

We have no need to dream of the mountains
Of home or the fall of water and its swirl
To the parting tides.

We are here, where the rock is sharp
Under our feet and the mat grass
Sways under the wind whirl.

We are here and may see hanging valleys
Gorge themselves on cloud and mist
And we listen everywhere to voices of water —
Now harped like glass strings over pebbles,
And then phrased, male-mouthed as a choir
For the shell trebled, skate-flown sea.

We can look with respect and easy affinity
Into the cooled magazine of the world,
Where Holly Fern and Rose-root and ice flowers
Hide in hollows (but not from us) and grip
Vice hard to ledges in the bracken gold of light
That tones this thunder-ripped bed of stone
Below the mew of buzzard.

We can stroke the slice of slate
And the temples of quartz,
Where the vixen's bark sends
The bleating through the ffridd
And the shallow soil drives flocks for miles
But, like us, they know the home ground
When the shepherd shrills a back flash
Of dog to the Crîb.

Stare through the streams where the sun
Hammers wedding rings on smooth anvils
And the hint of white water shapes
In the corner of your eye.

There are shells scalloped and spiralled
Into Snowdon, where the old folded seams
Heaved like sperm whales from the seabed,
And perched blocks rode limpet-back
To their salt cradles or stared as blind
Oriels and lancets in glazed minsters
Lurched to the monstrous cracking shore.

We of the mountains, streams and the Welsh sea
Of sunsets only leave them once — no more —
For we cannot bear the distant dreams.

T. Llewellyn Williams

WHEN IT'S OVER

Letter to S.S. from Mametz Wood, 1917

. . . there's a blue bay
Shining in front, and on the right
Snowdon and Hebog capped with white,
And lots of other jolly peaks
That you could wonder at for weeks,
With jag and spur and hump and cleft.
There's a grey castle on the left . . .

No traveller yet has hit upon
A wilder land than Meirion,
For desolate hills and tumbling stones,
Bogland and melody and old bones.
Fairies and ghosts are here galore,
And poetry most splendid, more
Than can be written with the pen
Or understood by common men.

In Gweithdy Bach we'll rest awhile,
We'll dress our wounds and learn to smile
With easier lips; we'll stretch our legs,
And live on bilberry tart and eggs,
And store up solar energy,
Basking in sunshine by the sea,
Until we feel a match once more
For *anything* but another war.

Robert Graves

DIRECTIONS FOR VISITORS

If you want to see Wales,
measure the long isosceles
of Snowdon with your feet;
fly your heart through the dappled trees
of calm Cwm Cynfal; dip
your finger-tips into the lees

of the old religion
at Holywell — and see the new
at pink Llantrisant mint.
Ascend the sacred avenue
of Strata Florida:
beyond the transept seek the yew,

the flame of evergreen
that streams up from dead Dafydd's bones,
and know that there, under
the sheep-cropped turf and tumbled stones,
are clenched the corded roots
stronger than new pence or old thrones.

Raymond Garlick

POSTCARD FROM LLANRWST

I don't want another night like that again.
There were three of us in this room,
A small room, too. And a dog
Bought seventeen years ago for the gun
And still hunting rabbits in his sleep,
And all the weather in Wales pressed down
On the Conway valley, squeezing out thunder,
Lightning, heavy rain, the lot.
Wara teg though, the view was interesting.
Too interesting, if anything: the Gwydir Chapel
Window to window with us, almost.
It isn't everyone who can go to bed
With a full view of Llewelyn Fawr's coffin.
Next morning I went to pay my respects
To the empty sarcophagus.
There were also present
Two lawnmowers and a milking stool.

Harri Webb

WELSH LOVE LETTER

Were all the peaks of Gwynedd
In one huge mountain piled,
Cnicht on Moelwyn,
Moel-y-gest, Moel Hebog,
And Eryri on top,
And all between us,
I'd climb them climb them
All!
To reach you.
O, how I love you!

Were all the streams of Gwynedd
In one great river joined,
Dwyfor, Dwyryd,
Glaslyn, Ogwen,
And Mawddach in flood,
And all between us,
I'd swim them swim them
All!
To reach you.
O, how I love you!

Were all the forts of Gwynedd
In one great fortress linked,
Caer and castle,
Criccieth, Harlech,
Conwy, Caernarfon,
And all in flames,
I'd jump them jump them
All!
To reach you.
O, how I love you!

See you Saturday,
If it's not raining.

Michael Burn

QUARRIES AT DINORWIC

1. The Hill

This is the black mountain
labour unpacked
so much, so long, it might have
built it:

ziggurat of terraces

precipitous pilgrimage of z-bend paths

poised avalanche of scree

fissile mud-stone home of the ancient, still-perfect

    segmented trilobite

wall and roof

the industrial history of a region

metamorphic headstone of a village.

Mile-high litter
of slate.

2. The Workshops

The converted museum of its foot is still
positivistic for an occasional public
of holiday-makers and sixth-form groups:
as if the past were what is finished with.

Its old slate blocks are the green
of the mountain's lake.

Inside, a fetishisation of the primitive
pauses you
in workshops of used paraphernalia:
patterns, hammers, saxes, saws;
the broad, unique chisels;
the geometrical rectangled edge
of slates cropped by two single, expert blows.

Even the machinery has been made gentle
by the wear of palms.

Nostalgia too, in the old photograph, mist-bleak
of ruffian labourers
on the rubbish of shalings outside
their rubble hut.
A xeroxed newspaper text still speaks
of them, defunct,
of their defunct, particular skills
with parochial pride.

Now all this remains
to the tourist,
who is inheriting the earth:
a museum of dead
shops whose air was once dense,
smoke-acrid with breathable motes
and, outside, the leaning
slag-heap
of all they didn't finally carry away
in those rusty iron trolleys
or the intricateness
of the astonishing, pink lung.

3. *The Graveyard in Dinorwic*

Here things change slower than the yew-trees,

and the village's graveyard, steep as Boot Hill, still
shows in ranks
the rank of its dead:

a massive, glassy granite urn;
one blind, white angel
like the Niké on a Rolls; the plinths
and obelisks of vaults
guarded by railing spears . . .

Mostly, though, the cluttered, ordinary
headstones, all facing one way —
oblongs or Gothic-arch-shapes: slabbed slate
from the black hill.

Sometimes, to live in Wales is to know
that the dead still outnumber the living.

The chisel put your names in the blue slabs.
Wandering among them, I
taste only your anonymity,
vicarious, bitter as brass —
accumulated
generations penned in
this village boneyard, herded
stones . . .

The chisel serifed your ages in the slate, too —
men dead in their 40s, the widows who outwaited them
for twenty years
by looking at the wall.

It was the slate put you here.

The slate that can now never be wiped clean.

Duncan Bush

CHWAREL BETHESDA: PETER PRENDERGAST

You set your table, bench and drawing board
On the quarry's edge and reach across
With eye and brush, to the far boundary
Between grazing and slate where a farmhouse waits
Above the drop that's swallowed its neighbours,
And a river, guillotined at the workface,
Stepladders down walls, terraces and slabs
Of seabed and estuary banked in stone
Till it reaches the bottom of this inside-out mountain.

No men and no machinery
Are at work in your painting.
There's only the shape they've made
Making a living from slate
By increments of poverty and profit.

Quarry huts, a ruined hawthorn,
The sky's muddy deposits.
Two miles towards the coast,
And out of the picture,
In his cut-out castle among trees,
While a *bwrdd naddu* sits idle in the early Silurian,
George Sholto Douglas Pennant, the owner,
Pours out a glass of Malvern water
And decides not to answer
A letter from the strike committee.

Bryan Aspden

SLATE

Drawn from his fold on the mean mountain
the brittle man of Wales shuffles black dominoes
and builds, on the shards of his father's dreams,
this meaner mountain, where grieving winds

polish the grim sarcophagus at Blaenau Ffestiniog.
We watch — but from a decent distance — the
     dismembering
of another's way of life, hewn, sawn, split and split again
to a wafer thin, then leaving the man spitting the dust

of his own drear day, well entertained we drive away
past prim rhododendron mountains, to tea and toast
on a silver tray with damask cloth at Betws-y-Coed,
and ladies with trim white hair and brown moustaches.

Maurice Rutherford

CASTELL Y BERE

So many deaths under unfurling trees
or on banks where primrose makes us dizzy
after ten miles of mountain track —

a lamb's head clean as a toy, the beads
of its vertebrae picked smooth as hail maries,
hobby horse, head on a stake, Llywelyn
shorn of his coat to mother-smell an orphan
for the grieving ewe.

In the barn that other lamb
a husk in my hands, delicate and swift
as a chalk horse, its four hooves galloping
no-where forever in its attitude
of birth, stillborn on its journey, still
in the caul of its skin, not skeleton
but bas-relief, little sea-horse, womb-horse.

In the wood the jay's discarded robe,
barred-blue wing-feathers, fallen black arrows
of flight, breast-down cream, rose, terra cotta,
a quiver of feathers, a drop of fresh blood
in calm afternoon but no bird at all.

Then the kestrel on its back in torchlight
dead with Tonfannau's ghostly soldiery
in the deserted military camp.
On a concrete floor littered with glass
and owl-pellets, his royal feathers dressed
impeccably black and gold as heraldry.
His turned head is a skull, his breast
a seethe of hatching spiders.

Gillian Clarke

CASTELL Y BERE

Come inside, graveyard, to see your stones,
the stones that were full of meaning. When Llywelyn
uttered them, the populace strained their ears
and were warmed by their grey rhythms. Up here
they lie like sheep atop sheep,
sheep within sheep, in a motionless fold
throughout a land's winter. They do not say much,
the clichés of rocks that continue to gape,
their towers speaking old power's old threat
through winter within winter. Diverting; small sheep
like snowballs scaling silent walls,
and sticking to their shadow against the sky's carvings:
I would love to follow them, but below on the green
I find a scene that suffices. At last, one
of the government ministries has rearranged
the stones neatly with ladders for tourists
to climb inside. . . . We'll dare to speak a bit louder.

Bobi Jones

(Translated by Joseph P. Clancy)

A BALLAD OF GLYN DŴR'S RISING

My son, the mist is clearing and the moon will soon be high,
And then we'll hear the thudding hooves, the horsemen
    speeding by,
With murmurs coming nearer, carried over on the breeze
Of the men who march in secret through the cloisters of the trees:
Tonight we two go riding, for the threads of fate are spun,
And we join Glyn Dŵr at Corwen at the rising of the sun.

For yesterday our leader was proclaimed the Prince of Wales,
His call to arms is sounding now among the hills and vales,
And Owain, heir of dynasties, in this auspicious year
May be our great deliverer, foretold by bard and seer:
And rumour runs that Arthur's voice is heard along the west
Acclaiming this descendant of Cadwaladr the Blest.

At last shall I unsheath again my father's two-edged sword,
And hand you mine to strike amain at Ruthin's tyrant lord,
Because I've waited, waited long throughout the bitter years
For this hour of freedom's challenge and the flashing of the
    spears:
So now we two must face as one the hazards of the night
To pledge our lives to Owain at the breaking of the light.

My son, go kiss your mother, kiss her gently, she'll not wake,
For an older mother calls you, though you perish for her sake:
The fabled Dragon banner flies once more above the Dee
Where the sons of Wales are gathering to set our people free
From wrong and dire oppression: pray, my son, for strength
    anew,
For widows will be weeping at the falling of the dew.

A.G. Prys-Jones

DEFEAT IN THE NORTH

The spent horses droop across the marram,
their hooves sinking in it. Down the sheep-runs
bleating flocks scatter before them.
All day the useless pack-mules tramp the ridge
coming back from the fight, swarms of flies at their heads;
the foot-soldiers stumble behind,
lice crawling in their jerkins.

Carts of wounded are lodged in sand.
The camp women have gone with the foreign king
and his rabble. By lakeshore and deep bog
peasants milk cows and thatch roofs
as stragglers stump into the hills
while a nation dies before cock-crow.
The foreign commander in his bright cape and hat
looks down from the ridge. He is confident
that his Sovereign Lord, Henry, by the Grace of God,
the Fourth of that name, will approve.
'They put up a good fight.'
He wheels about, trots back to his supper and bed.

A horn blows clear in an upland pass.
It is the fatal moment for a dipped flag,
for the old grudging earth of Gwynedd.
Blades and cudgels lie in the fields
as rain drizzles down through the night
and smoke from the doused turf fires
drifts across silent Beddgelert.
A few horsemen cover the prince's start for Fflint
when he rides away from his *hafod*,
a thin beard on his chin and his eyes sharp.
He turns in the saddle, against the skyline
and lifts one arm to stretch his cloak
in farewell salute. His soldiers watch him
bold against the sky, riding away . . .

John Tripp

41

ODE

I love a fine-built fort in a crescent of hills,
where a proud form breaks into my sleep.
A notable, resolute man will get through to it,
the savage, vocal wave howls to it,
chosen place of a beauty whose qualities shine.
Bright and shining it rises from the ocean shore
to the woman who shines upon this year.
A year in Snowdonia, in desolate Arfon:
no one who deserves a pavilion or a silk mantle
do I love more than I love her.
If she granted her favour in return for my verse,
I would be next to her every night.

Hywel ab Owain Gwynedd

(Translated by Gwyn Williams)

SONNET: COMPOSED AMONG THE RUINS OF A CASTLE IN NORTH WALES

(September 1824)

Through shattered galleries, 'mid roofless halls,
Wandering with timid footsteps oft betrayed,
The Stranger sighs, nor scruples to upbraid
Old Time, though he, gentlest among the Thralls
Of Destiny, upon these wounds hath laid
His lenient touches, soft as light that falls,
From the wan Moon, upon the towers and walls,
Light deepening the profoundest sleep of shade,
Relic of Kings! Wreck of forgotten wars,
To winds abandoned and the prying stars,
Time *loves* Thee! at his call the Seasons twine
Luxuriant wreaths around thy forehead hoar;
And, though past pomp no changes can restore,
A soothing recompense, his gift, is thine!

William Wordsworth

CASTLE

On the tour the old guide showed us
the great banqueting hall where they feasted
off huge chops, swan, venison, brandy wine;
and the bedrooms where they enjoyed incest,
breeding simpletons to keep it in the family
and a name on the enormous maps.
    A priest was kept at the back
    on a pallet and ration of wine
    to bless killers off to Jerusalem.

Then we saw the dungeons' slimed walls
with rack, screws, brazier and rusted manacles
where they cut off tongues and put out eyes.
    When kings held a Christmas court,
the baying of hounds and the squawking of chickens
blotted out the screams from downstairs.

It was all log-fires then —
wood, stone, leather, hide and sheepskin
in turrets of fatal draught, the women tough as boots
through marriages of freezing utility.

The guide didn't mention the smells and disease,
or the rats, the battalions of cockroaches.
    Or the intelligence
of corkscrew lords, devious in the bone.
Or the dark and endless boredom
when those lovely, tall, fat, twelve-day candles
    red-numeral-marked in sections
    night by night sank into their wax . . .

John Tripp

LANDSCAPE: NORTH WALES

There is a tree standing bare as a pencil,
Holding the eye like a cross.
There is the road like a river
And rivers like slow worms squirming
Their way round stone and root.
One must have a farmhouse
Looking tired and snail-small
Against the stirring cauldron of the mountains,
And from it slate and rock walls
Numb through stretching to hold the cold land.
Sheep are essential; never more than ten,
Suffering their way by rock, moss and weed.
Lastly (though not essential) a man
May be seen to lumber at the tree,
Pull grey, autumn-speckled trout
From the streams before the quick falls
And crop his rooted sheep that chew down
The hours, leaving berries of dung
To face the tired moving of the sun.

Tony Curtis

LANDSCAPE: NORTH WALES (RE-CONSIDERED)

I take it back —
There is a tree standing bare as a pencil!
for today at Bala there is a wonder of trees;
sun seeps through a tangle of branches,
works an alchemy of gold and bronze
against the green,
wears Summer's fern to rust.
This road leads somewhere:
past the water's slow curve,
an angler propped at the edge
outstaring the lake's patience;
on a day where winds of Eastern wars
— the tight grin aching through sand into skull —
die;
and blue-clouded Aran Benllyn
holds promise of fresh weather,
then carries the eye far out
over Aran Fawddwy to the opening West
where a jet's chalky path already reaches sea.

Tony Curtis

DEFENCE OF THE WEST

Interceptors over Gwynedd

Talking to the shepherd, my eyes
kept on his ginger stubble
and a Woodbine jammed in a hole
in his upper teeth
(it's not often you meet someone who can do that).
He scratched the dog with his stick.
My boots slithered in the muck,
it was cold and his breath plumed
as he spoke of sheep and weather
with the nous of centuries behind him.

At first it was a far-off buzz, a sort of
hiss. 'Here they come,' he said.
We stopped talking and listened.
Then out of the west beyond a lattice
of trees, pummelling the ground,
came the hunters suddenly above us
screaming as they bullet-streaked
across the morning sky —
slide-rule perfection in itself
headed out to Menai and the sea.

Two swept over, then one, sluggish
like a slower younger son
still testing its speed; you could see
red-and-white dicing on the nose.
In seconds they had gone
and the trees stopped shaking;
the silence was full of vibrations.

I looked from the sky
to the shepherd, his thin face nutbrown
from years of coastal wind, a weak smile

seaming it as he glanced around the fields.
'They were shifting,' I said.
He lowered the fag to his bottom lip.
'That's progress for you,' he said.

John Tripp

HORSES

Suddenly there were forms there:
Heads bright of eye
Leapt out of the alien dark,
Out of the night into the headlights' gleam.

The twentieth century braked
And in the tousled manes before us
Pieces out of the past were
Gazing at us brightly.

Neighing and snorting nostrils,
Legs teeming with terror;
Scattering then. After the hooves
Stopped threshing the darkness: stillness.

After the nerves of seeing
Stopped twitching with the imprint of the flurry
Of the forms that came before our faces
Like a fist, the light was full of quietness.

Shifting into gear and moving
On a road that wound along the face of the world
In a wide night where time was untied
And let loose in a fearful roaming.

Gwyn Thomas

(Translated by Joseph P. Clancy)

HEATHER

They grow so comely, a quiet host, fine gems
Of the shire of sun and breeze,
Bells hanging from high rock places,
Flowers of the stone, phials of honey.

Eifion Wyn

(Translated by Tony Conran)

SNOWDONIA NATIONAL PARK

This was the fortress of all ancient dreams,
Where princes played, with kingdoms for the stake,
At games of hazard, pledging pass and lake
With Norman brokers; when they lost, it seems,
Their creditors annexed the pawned estate,
And as new landlords proved a greater ill
Since lawlessness could best their coffers fill;
Always were blood and death sad Gwynedd's fate.
It has not changed; still the dark legends cling
To moor and mountain in the ravished land;
In the broad plain Rhiannon's birds still sing,
And nameless lords lie slaughtered close at hand.
Is this your park? Indeed a fitting name
With which to mark a land of this red fame!

Sally Roberts Jones

A WELSH WORDSCAPE 1

To live in Wales,

Is to be mumbled at
by re-incarnations of Dylan Thomas
in numerous diverse disguises.

Is to be mown down
by the same words
at least six times a week.

Is to be bored
by Welsh visionaries
with wild hair and grey suits.

Is to be told
of the incredible agony
of an exile
that can be at most
a day's travel away.

And the sheep, the sheep,
the bloody flea-bitten Welsh sheep,
chased over the same hills
by a thousand poetic phrases
all saying the same things.

To live in Wales
is to love sheep
and to be afraid
of dragons.

Peter Finch

The Lakes

THE QUIET LAKE

Quiet as a lawn under sunlight,
as an undersea landscape.

Quiet as a cloudless sky,
as a girl sleeping.

Quiet as a blue heaven,
as a trout in the water's shade under the bridge
immobile.

Quiet as a clear mirror,
as a dream between hopes.

Quiet as seeing from a plane
a deep forest
and a gold river running through it.

Quiet as a wood-pigeon brooding on the rooftop,
as starlings tidy
between two posts of an electric cable.

Quiet as Ceridwen's Cauldron before the seething,
as Llyn y Fan Fach before the maiden rose.

Quiet as Owain Glyn Dŵr's tomb
between the stars' hedgerows,
as Cantre'r Gwaelod
astir in the ear.

Quietness
a vibrancy,
like awaiting a high wind.

Euros Bowen

(Translated by Joseph P. Clancy)

LLYN TEGID (BALA LAKE)

Strange that something as unmountainous as this
Wandered into the land. Once in a while it pretends
That it isn't there, that it's only a continuation of the slopes;
But, another time, the nature of its lineage will come into
      view
In leaping teeth and passion-white locks,
As it tosses itself towards the strand
As if bent on escaping. A lake is a stranger,
Not belonging to the ancient place despite the weaving of
      centuries.
How often it turns its eyes, full of dream,
Away from here, a too-lonely pilgrim, its heart
Yearning in narrow-whorled agonies down
Through the valleys to the sea, to the unfailing nest
Of complete community, the entertainment, the
      excitement, and the infinite.
In crannied pools by the shore it imagines
It senses the terrible uproar of the wave and the perilous
      scent of the seaweed.
No pillow, no roots, no wishing to fuse
Into its sinful brown uncongenial soil,
It lodges here for a while among rocky places;
And upon its ear breaks a crisp tranquil breeze from the
      heather
Telling lies like wine about earth's charm.

Bobi Jones

(Translated by Joseph P. Clancy)

LLYN Y GADAIR

The jaunty traveller that comes to peer
Across its shallows to the scene beyond
Would almost not see it. Mountains here
Have far more beauty than this bit of pond
With one man fishing in a lonely boat
Whipping the water, rowing now and then
Like a poor errant wretch, condemned to float
The floods of nightmare never reaching land.

But there's some sorcerer's bedevilling art
That makes me see a heaven in its face,
Though glory in that aspect has no part
Nor on its shore is any excelling grace —
Nothing but peat bog, dead stumps brittle and brown,
Two crags and a pair of quarries, both closed down.

T.H. Parry-Williams

(Translated by Tony Conran)

CWMORTHIN

Here the cliffs come together,
Here the cliffs share a secret and draw
Close to each other, stand shoulder to shoulder:
Here is a cup of loneliness.

The cwm lies in an ancient mountain,
And there's a lake between the rock scars
And old heaps of slates that were rolled into it
When times were prosperous.
Everyone has gone now
Leaving behind them the marks of habitation —
Iron wheels, their teeth rusty, on their backs
Like terrible old mouths, old jaws of whales;
Old eyeless ruins, like empty skulls
Here and there, and an old chapel in decay.
The great mountain and its long silence reclaim them.
Everything goes back to the indifference of rock,
To the grasp of the grass and the sedges, to the water's
        blackness,
Under the barren sky.

The cliff's old age, the abyss of days,
The motionless elements' age, the rock and its veins
Open a great void.
Here one sees to the cleft of the years.
Here one sees the stillness of time.

Emptiness, emptiness, emptiness.
In the emptiness of the place, in the emptiness of the season
Under the vast sky
Is a lake in a cup of loneliness.

Gwyn Thomas

(Translated by Joseph P. Clancy)

LOCALITY

Croak of the raven will echo from Pendist Mawr
On Snowdon's slopes when I fight with the Giant Death.

And weeping from Nant-y-Betws and Drws-y-Coed
And from Cae'r-Gors bridge when the verdict is announced.

A scar will crease the face of Llyn Cwellyn, and on
Llyn y Gadair too wrinkles that weren't there before.

A crack will appear on the schoolhouse by the road
When the news is told to the listening telephone.

A crick will contract Eryri and through the flow
Of Gwyrfai river the cramp of my death will creep.

This is not a mere madman's fantasy-thinking —
There are bits of me scattered all over that land.

T.H. Parry-Williams

(Translated by R. Gerallt Jones)

AWEN: PARC LAKE, CONWY VALLEY

This lake with the pines around it,
This pure globe,
Brimming at last, by gravity drawn down,
Leaps in a serious frenzy
To the plain.

Soon tasting salt
Moves out against the tide,
Yet finds no force,
Made idle in these acres where the marsh,
Shallow and brackish,
Hides only foundation lines
Of the ploughed and salted city.

In sun the marsh mists rise:
Brine burns the weeds,
The river fails.

Next spring again the snows,
Melting, will hurl the lake towards that sea.

Sally Roberts Jones

PENMAEN POOL

For the Visitors' Book at the Inn

Who long for rest, who look for pleasure
Away from counter, court, or school
O where live well your lease of leisure
But here at, here at Penmaen Pool?

You'll dare the Alp? you'll dart the skiff? —
Each sport has here its tackle and tool:
Come, plant the staff by Cadair cliff;
Come, swing the sculls on Penmaen Pool.

What's yonder? — Grizzled Dyphwys dim:
The triple-hummocked Giant's Stool,
Hoar messmate, hobs and nobs with him
To halve the bowl of Penmaen Pool.

And all the landscape under survey,
At tranquil turns, by nature's rule,
Rides repeated topsyturvy
In frank, in fairy Penmaen Pool.

And Charles's Wain, the wondrous seven,
And sheep-flock clouds like worlds of wool,
For all they shine so, high in heaven,
Shew brighter shaken in Penmaen Pool.

The Mawddach, how she trips! though throttled
If floodtide teeming thrills her full,
And mazy sands all water-wattled
Waylay her at ebb, past Penmaen Pool.

But what's to see in stormy weather,
When grey showers gather and gusts are cool?
Why, raindrop-roundels looped together
That lace the face of Penmaen Pool.

Then even in weariest wintry hour
Of New Year's month or surly Yule
Furred snows, charged tuft above tuft, tower
From darksome darksome Penmaen Pool.

And ever, if bound here hardest home,
You've parlour-pastime left and (who'll
Not honour it?) ale like goldy foam
That frocks an oar in Penmaen Pool.

Then come who pine for peace or pleasure
Away from counter, court, or school,
Spend here your measure of time and treasure
And taste the treats of Penmaen Pool.

Gerard Manley Hopkins

WHEN THE WIND

When the wind is green,
Seaweed in the sea,
The flesh of the ivy,
And the glass in the windows of the lake.

When the wind is yellow.
The sand and the seashells,
Chorales of the daffodil,
And the moon on the lake's floor.

When the wind is red,
Far out at sea,
Oats and apples,
And fires lighting up in the lake.

And when the wind is black,
And the sun hidden
In the cellars of the lake,
I will find the thing which was lost.

Euros Bowen

(Translated by R. Gerallt Jones)

SAILING

It was very strange to watch him sail
Away from me on the calm water,
The white sail duplicate. I knew
All the people in the boat and felt
The tightening lines of my involvement.

My children were in the boat, and my friends,
And he in the stern. The sheet of water
Thinned between us as he sailed away.
I strolled on the path and waved
And felt in the space a terrible desolation.

When they returned the exhilaration
Of the familiar morning had gone. I felt
As though on the water he had found
New ways of evasion, a sheet
Of icy water to roll out between us.

Gillian Clarke

OWL

Back home in Arfon, with nothing but the sound
Of the wind and the river and the lake's small ripple,
And sometimes the busybody bark of a hound,
Sudden and harsh, as someone crosses the hill;
Back home in Arfon, why should I make it my
Concern, whatever king may do or crank,
Or fear oppressors' frowns? Never has the cry
Of the base world come over the top of the bank . . .
As night closed in, boldly, without a care,
I strolled along the highway all alone,
Counting the pitch-black poles, each in a pair,
And the trilling wires, each one by one;
Between a prop and a pole, on a round pipe,
I saw an owl, — and felt terror's grip.

T.H. Parry-Williams

(Translated by Joseph P. Clancy)

SHEEPDOG

Smooth steps that are easy to urge to the crags
    And inaccessible places;
Gathering and halving flocks
Is his exploit in far glens.

Thomas Richards

(Translated by Tony Conran)

TRYWERYN

'Nothing's gone that matters — a dozen farms,
A hollow of no great beauty, scabby sheep,
A gloomy Bethel and a field where sleep
A few dead peasants. There are finer charms
Observed in rising water, as its arms
Circle and meet above the walls; in cheap
Power and growing profits. Who could reap
Harvests as rich as this in ploughmen's palms?
All's for the best — rehoused, these natives, too,
Should bless us for sanitation and good health.
Later, from English cities, see the view
Misty with hiraeth — and their new-built wealth.'

'All of our wealth's in men — and their life's blood
Drawn from the land this water drowns in mud'.

Sally Roberts Jones

CLYWEDOG

The people came out in pairs,
Old, most of them, holding their places
Close till the very last minute,
Even planting the beans as usual
That year, grown at last accustomed
To the pulse of the bulldozers.
High in those uphill gardens, scarlet
Beanflowers blazed hours after
The water rose in the throats of the farms.

Only the rooted things stayed:
The wasted hay, the drowned
Dog roses, the farms, their kitchens silted
With their own stones, hedges
And walls a thousand years old.
And the mountains, in a head-collar
Of flood, observe a desolation
They'd grown used to before the coming
Of the wall-makers. Language
Crumbles to wind and bird-call.

Gillian Clarke

MARCHLYN

I no longer believe in Arthur.

I believed (like all loyal Arthurians
of the Arfon denomination) that
he was buried beneath Marchlyn,
the kingliest and most mysterious lake in Gwynedd.
I also believed he would rise again
and lead us all (all Welsh-speaking
men of Gwynedd, that is) to victory.

But the ground, as it were, of my belief
has been shifted: McAlpines have drained the lake.
The steel monsters that have defiled his grave
have not dredged up one murmur of dissent
from Arthur.

Can he be frightened by a horde of Irishmen?
Or is it even worse than that? —
Perhaps he's actually in league with them:
for when the desecration is complete
they're going to replace the lake,
neatly landscaped,
and up McAlpines' new road will come
bright busloads of comfortable pilgrims
straight from the Dragon Routes.

But, try as I might, I can't accept
a King who's joined the Wales Tourist Board:
not *there* lies victory!

Of course, he may have left,
not quite having slept enough yet.
The last time I went to look for a sign,
the Blue Knight at the gate barred my way,
saying: 'We are empowered to stop anyone from coming in —

though we can't stop anyone from going out'
and tapped, cunningly, the motto 'Securicor'
emblazoned on his helmet.
So Arthur may have slunk off,
disguised as a stray rambler,
his crown hidden in his rucksack.

Ian Hughes

THE FLOODED VALLEY

Under the lake's press:
rock, bone, grasses;
the soft slime
of moss and fern;

a road plunges
into the water,
winds, traces the contours
of the depths.

Swim down its cleft,
walk the length
of the sunken river
past trees wintered by water.

What can you find?
What signs are recognised?

A fish netted by
the twisted branches
of a high pine.
Its spine flaps.

A dog-fox clamped
by its leg in a gin.
Time wearing away the snout,
baring teeth into tight grin.

A low, stone church:
fish curl around the cross,
water moves the bell
tolling the silent hours.

Enter the church,
the fish turn
expectantly
for your Word.

Tony Curtis

THIS ONE

What do I care about Wales? It's just an odd chance
That I live on her land. All she is on a map

Is a sliver of earth in an off-beat corner,
Just a nuisance to those who believe in order.

And who lives in this backwater, just tell me that?
The refuse of humanity; for God's sake, don't

Cackle about entities, nations and countries;
Plenty of those, leave out Wales, around in the world.

I'm fed up long since of the strange caterwauling
Of these Welshmen, Lord, keeping up their complaining.

I'll be off, away from their speeches and writings,
Back to my childhood haunts; my fancy will take me.

And here I am. Thank goodness I'm finally lost,
Far from the clamouring words of all extremists.

There's Snowdon and its crew; here's the bare, naked land;
Here's the lake and the river and crag; to be sure,

Here's where I was born. But see, between earth and sky,
There are voices and phantoms in all these places.

I'm uncertain, and now, I don't mind telling you,
I feel a kind of weakness creeping over me,

And the claws of Wales clutching, torturing my breast,
God preserve me, I cannot escape from this one.

T.H. Parry-Williams

(Translated by R. Gerallt Jones)

SENTENCES WHILE REMEMBERING HIRAETHOG

It was a summer evening
they were all there
oh I remember them I tell you

old people that are this scorching hour
no more than tattered lips in the wind
and the others
the red-ripe hearts
with their laughter in fragments amongst the reeds
and their hair unkempt

where are the buttermilk voices that used to flow
through the kitchen and the dairy and the cowshed
and the laughter in fragments among the reeds

where are the round eyes
that disappeared in a cloud of laughter

I prayed that I might be one of the colts
on the Oerfa mountain for ever
it would be damned cold in winter of course
said Jo laughingly
odd that his voice that minute was like a bell

It was a summer evening
they were all there
the wind idly meandered through the corn

oh I remember them I tell you.

T. Glynne Davies

(Translated by R. Gerallt Jones)

THE SWAN

Today the art of our retreat
Is to see portents and mystery —
To see colour and sinew, the flash of white
As the bare hills of the age are visited from heaven:
His solitude swims in the quiet of the water,
A pilgrim acquainted with sedges,
And he washes the weather of the lake with his form
That (as it were) spotlights the passion
Of a soul's breath
As it goes its slow, bare way in the chill of March:
His neck became a vigil,
The immaculate arm of a hunter,
The poise there, the stance of his eye! —
And the flame of his beak plummeted down to the pool:
The mountains looked disquieted
As he resumed his glide, easing himself to the flood:
A shiver ran through his wings, then stopped,
And on a sharp beat he broke from the water:
Slowly he went, then up to the high air,
And the fire of his wings draws a soul from its cold.

Euros Bowen

(Translated by Tony Conran)

BY LLYN OGWEN

Two hours ago the mountains were blackcapped like a
        hanging judge,
and the winds wrestled in an aerial dogfight
tearing the low clouds in shreds flying and wheeling,
and the lower slopes were a backdrop of brown
over the slate-coloured lake.

But now the sun is a god of victory
exulting over his kingdom of immense
hills, and his paraclete blesses and illumines
their slopes in sharp light and deep shadows,
and the stream, earlier a lead-coloured cleft in the field,
sparkles like a glass necklace.

I can understand how simpler men in simpler ages
saw the sun as a great god charioting the heavens,
and I could easily believe at this moment
that God rode in a golden cart, shaping, reshaping
the whole of this vast valley in his hands.

Frederic Vanson

LAKE

A breeze strokes the mane
of this water.
Like some mirror in an old tale
the picture waves and folds
and reforms again.
Day by day
moment by moment,
the story writes itself on the water,
the clouds, the stony faces
of the mountains,
the blue tent that is all
we know of heaven.

This lake is an eye
that never blinks or sleeps.
You can walk from this shore,
soar on whatever winds you care
to catch, tread on whatever paths cross
the water's skin,
because this will be only
the illusion of action,
the passing glint of light in
the chalice,
no more than your dreams
in the eye of water.
In the open eye of water.

Tony Curtis

The Coastline

THE SEAGULL

A fine gull on the tideflow,
All one white with moon or snow,
Your beauty's immaculate,
Shard like the sun, brine's gauntlet.
Buoyant you're on the deep flood,
A proud swift bird of fishfood.
You'd ride at anchor with me,
Hand in hand there, sea lily.
Like a letter, a bright earnest,
A nun you're on the tide's crest.

Right fame and far my dear has —
Oh, fly round tower and fortress,
Look if you can't see, seagull,
One bright as Eigr on that wall.
Say all my words together.
Let her choose me. Go to her.
If she's alone — though profit
With so rare a girl needs wit —
Greet her then: her servant, say,
Must, without her, die straightway.

She guards my life so wholly —
Ah friends, none prettier than she
Taliesin or the flattering lip
Or Merlin loved in courtship:
Cypris courted 'neath copper,
Loveliness too perfect-fair.

Seagull, if that cheek you see,
Christendom's purest beauty,
Bring to me back fair welcome
Or that girl must be my doom.

Dafydd ap Gwilym

(Translated by Tony Conran)

THE SEAGULL

Fair gull on the water's bank,
Bright-plumed breast, well-provided,
Hawk does not seize or pursue,
Water drown, nor man own you.
Nun feasting on the ocean,
Green sea's corners' coarse-voiced girl,
Thrusting wide through the lake's neck;
And then shaking a herring,
Salt water's clear white sunlight,
You're the banner of the shore.
The blessed godchild are you,
Below the bank, of Neptune:
A sorrow for you, the change
Of your life, cold your christening,
Brave white bird in rough waters,
Once a girl in a man's arms.

Halcyon, fair slim-browed maiden,
You were called in your kind land,
And after your man, good cause,
To the waves then you ventured,
And to the wild strait's seagull
You were changed, weak-footed bird.
You live, quick fish-feeding girl,
Below the slope and billows,
And the same cry for your mate
You screech loudly till doomsday.

Was there ever on the sea
A more submissive swimmer?
Hear my cry, wise and white-cloaked,
The hurt of the bare sea's bard:
My breast is pained with passion,
Pining for love of a girl.

I have begged from my boyhood
That she'd make one tryst with me,
And the tryst was for today:
Great was grief, it was wasted.
Swim, forget not my complaint,
To the dear maiden's region;
Fly to the shore, brave brightness,
And say where I was held fast
By the mouth, no gentle wave,
Of rough Bermo, cold foaming,
In all moods a sorry spot,
A cold black sea for sailing.

I rose, I travelled as day was
Breaking towards that dear bright face.
Dawn came on a thorny seastrand,
A cold day from the south-east.
A foul wind winnowed gravel,
Stripping stones, the whirlwind's nest.
The signs grew darker with dawn,
Twrch Trwydd drenching the beaches.
Inky was the wind's gullet
Where the western wind draws breath.

Harsh is the shore in conflict
If the western inlet's rough:
The sea spews, turning rocks green,
From the east spews fresh water.
Deep heaves from the ocean-bed,
In pain the pale moon's swooning.
The green pond is heaved abroad,
A snake's heave, sick from surfeit.
Sad heave where I saw tide ebb,
Rain's drivel that came pouring,

Cold black bed between two slopes,
Salt-filled briny sea-water.
Furnace dregs, draff of hell-spit,
Mouth sucking drops from the stars,

A winter night's greedy mouth,
Greed on the face of night-time,
Crock-shaped wet-edged enclosure,
A ban between bard and girl,
Foul hollow gap, raging pit,
Foggy land's filthy cranny,
Cromlech of every sickness,
Narrow pit of the world's plagues.
The pit was the sea-pool's haunt,
High it leaped, pool of prickles.
As high as the shelf it climbs,
Spew of the storm-path's anguish.
It never ebbs, will not turn:
I could not cross the current.

Three waters could flow eastwards,
Three oceans, these are the ones:
The Euxin, where rain wets us,
The Adriatic, black look,
The flood that runs to Rhuddallt,
Ancient Noah's flood turned salt.
The water-gate at Bermo,
Tide and shelf, may it turn land!

Siôn Phylip

(*Translated by Joseph P. Clancy*)

YOUNG FELLOW FROM LLŶN

Young fellow from Llŷn, who's the girl of your heart,
You who wander so late in the evening apart?
My sweetheart is young and she comes from the Sarn,
And neat is her cottage that's under the Garn.

And what does she look like, the girl of your heart,
You who wander so late in the evening apart?
Dark, dark is my darling and dark haired is she,
But white shines her body like foam on the sea.

And what is she wearing, the girl of your heart,
You who wander so late in the evening apart?
In a long gown of shining white satin she goes
And red in her bosom there blushes a rose.

Young fellow from Llŷn, is she angry and flown,
That you wander so late in the evening alone?
Oh, never my sweetheart showed anger or pride
Since the very first time that we walked side by side.

Young fellow from Llŷn, why do tears then start
To your eyes as you wander so late and apart?
From her cheek Death has withered the roses away
And white is the wear in the cottage of clay.

William Jones

(Translated by Harri Webb)

ISLANDMAN

Full of years and seasoned like a salt timber
The island fisherman has come to terms with death.
His crabbed fingers are coldly afire with phosphorous
From the night-sea he fishes for bright-armoured herring.

Lifting his lobster pots at sunrise,
He is not surprised when drowned sailors
Wearing ropes of pearl round green throats,
Nod their heads at him from underwater forests.

His black-browed wife who sits at home
Before the red hearth, does not guess
That only a fishscale breastplate protects him
When he sets out across ranges of winter sea.

Brenda Chamberlain

THE FISHERMAN

Land speaks to him
Out beyond the islands:
You belong to me.

As he grows older, its beckoning
Becomes insistent. Walking the shore
For his nets, the wet sand blue
And scudding white with winter sky,
He leaves no prints. And yet
The gravestones at his back
Are the black wicks
Of his identity; the names on them
Outstare the tide. Hearing
The wind howl, its open mouth
Pressed against the window where he sits
To weld his lobster pots
Or coiling ropes, he's sure
His feet demand the firm horizons.
One more season; then the farm
Can home him and enfold him,
Warm with certainties.

Only, the sea longs
To lick
And lick him smooth.
His boat is turned
For harbour, but all day, inland,
He tastes the salt
That tightens on his mouth.

Christine Evans

EXULTATION

A foaming white wave washes over a grave,
the tomb of Rhufawn Pebyr, regal chieftain.
I love today what the English hate, the open land of the North,
and the varied growth that borders the Lliw.
I love those who gave me my fill of mead
where the seas reach in long contention.
I love its household and its strong buildings
and at its lord's wish to go to war.
I love its strand and its mountains,
its castle near the woods and its fine lands,
its water meadows and its valleys,
its white gulls and its lovely women.
I love its soldiers, its trained stallions,
its woods, its brave men and its homes.
I love its fields under the little clover,
where honour was granted a secure joy.
I love its regions, to which valour entitles,
its wide waste lands and its wealth.
O, Son of God, how great a wonder,
how splendid the stags, great their possessions!
With the thrust of a spear I did splendid work
between the host of Powys and lovely Gwynedd.
On a pale white horse, a rash adventure,
may I now win freedom from my exile.
I'll never hold out till my people come;
a dream says so and God wills so.
A foaming white wave washes over a grave.
A white wave, near the homesteads, foams over,
coloured like hoar-frost in the hour of its advance.
I love the sea-coast of Meirionnydd,
where a white arm was my pillow,
I love the nightingale in the wild wood,
where two waters meet in that sweet valley.
Lord of heaven and earth, ruler of Gwynedd,
how far Kerry is from Caer Lliwelydd!

In Maelienydd I mounted on a bay
and rode night and day to Rheged.
May I have, before my grave, a new conquest,
the land of Tegeingl, fairest in the world.
Though I be a lover of Ovid's way,
may God be mindful of me at my end.
A white wave, near the homesteads, foams over.

Hywel ab Owain Gwynedd

(Translated by Gwyn Williams)

FROM EXILE

It's bright the icy foam as it flows,
It's fierce in January great sea tumult,
It's woe's me the language, long-wished-for speech
For the sake of tales, would be sweet to my ear.

Ability in English I never had,
Neither knew phrases of passionate French:
A stranger and foolish, when I've asked questions
It turned out crooked — I spoke North Welsh!

On a wave may God's son grant us our wish
And out from amongst them readily bring us
To a Wales made one, contented and fair,
To a prince throned, laden nobly with gifts,
To the lord of Dinorwig's bright citadel land,
To the country of Dafydd, where Welsh freely flows!

Dafydd Benfras

(Translated by Tony Conran)

DRIVING DOWN THE MAWDDACH

The spatter of homing lorry-drivers
cornering for sundown and the wife;
the publicised colours of autumn raging
across the valleys between lined
spruces and sheep-flocked screes;
a sense of drama, of strife

under redness of mountain-barriered sky.
Dolgellau solid-angled in black
stone smudged by smoke of unseen
warmth, the streets empty. Bontddu
balanced in architecture against well-judged
woodland, with a worrying lack
of foot movement, of life.

Down the wild infertile estuary
opening, though braceletted by
its bridge, to infinite awayness, the turn
to the hybrid town and seafront where
men will deny horizon and mountain
for legs of blonde girls, icecream and a Mercian cry.

Gwyn Williams

SLATE QUAY: FELINHELI

1

This will go too, this curve of shore
Which, bending the tangled Straits,
Looks over at fields that bulge smoothly
Under the folded church of Llanfairisgaer.

Today a brown clout of mist rushes
Over the grey, brawling waters.
The trees bow in anticipation
Curled by the wind's clinical hands
For the sudden drilling rape of rain
On their pale-bellied leaves.

Here, in this village which is asleep
And has not awoken for hundreds of years,
On its blue and grey quayside
Swept of slate piles and inhabited
Now by tatty dogs, lone walkers
The strident gulls and suave
Motor-cruisers, the lives of men
Sing in moist air and the spirit
Of human life wanders, inconsolable,
Pitting a faded emphasis against the end.

2

The small dog which ran, paused, poised
Pissed on a bollard then tracked on swiftly
Has it all his own way.
The bridge waits for the axe
The locks leak and spurt
The arrogant yachts bump the wall
And look as if it were not there.

An old woman calls the dog which, deaf,
Maps out again its world of odours.

Two times are here but one will conquer
As the sleepwalking people
Twitch obediently to their till's song.

Peter Gruffydd

CROSSING A SHORE

It was, that day,
September the second.
And here we were, as a family,
Deciding to go to the sea.

It was, that day,
Sunny though a bit windy.
Over the great, empty shore
The wind would shake
The brightnesses of the sun,
Would whistle its yellow across the sand
And sparkle the water on the tide's far ebb.

And here we were, starting to do the things
That people do on beaches —
Shovel sand;
Put the baby to sit in the salty
Marvel of it; build castles; kick a ball.
The boys even went bathing
As though they'd a duty to.
But it was, that day,
Too cold to stay long in the water.
I just stood watching.

They came glistening out of the sea, their teeth
Chattering, laughing and splashing,
And here they were then, running in front of me
Across the long beach
To their mam, to their sister,
To shelter and towels.

I just followed at a distance.
But as I crossed the beach, about halfway,
It struck me with a shock
That this happens only once.

What I was doing would never, never come back.
Even the moment just gone
Is gripped within eternity
Fast as the Iron Age.
That's what it means, our mortality.
And I felt a bit lost then —
This thing won't ever happen again.

But I kept on walking
And before long I came back
To the family,
To the palaver of drying and changing,
To the sound of the present.
And what with digging the sand
And crunching through a tomato sandwich
And trying to calm the baby
That sense of loss went by.

I had, as it happened,
My birthday that day.
I was forty-one.

There's an old Russian proverb which says,
'Life is not crossing a field.'
Correct: it is crossing a shore.

Gwyn Thomas

(Translated by Tony Conran)

YOURS OF THE 29th

Why Lourdes, not Enlli? Both
no doubt are places where the earth's
crust is thin, and the world
of grace breaks through. The bedrock girths
are split, and through the dark
fissure refulgence, and rebirths

of limbs and lives, stream down
the serene and innocent air.
Beuno and Bernadette
both saw the true shape that was there,
wholeness and holiness
in form unutterably fair.

Why Lourdes, not Enlli then?
Not Enlli climbing in a cloud
of light from the green sea,
Enlli untouched, at peace, and loud
only with sea-birds' cries;
but admass Lourdes, light of the crowd,

spring in the concrete drought
of supermarket, one-way-street,
asylum, city square.
Today a man must go to greet
grace in this wilderness,
the cool cave in this desert's heat.

Raymond Garlick

BRYN CELLI DDU

Among the soil and stones, like an old dog,
Death has been gnawing at a bone
For three thousand years in Bryn Celli Ddu.

Until the sun was pick-axed into its depths
And time spaded off the skeletons,
And the grey shadows of an early race lay bare.

Mortality was not heard scuttling here
Crudely, frighteningly, angularly among the stones:
In the analysing of the darkness it quietly stole away.

And those who once walked Anglesey, their substance
    passed
Through the soil, green into the grass and shining into the
    water,
Their spirit was washed by the rain, the sun drank up their
    pain.

Their life was scattered in the wind,
Lost in the long time
Which stretches between us and that which once was.

Yet in our blood their being
Is a red secret sucking through our hearts,
A knot of life, a grip of recognition.

And we, poor things
Compared to the unpredictable power of death,
Pierce the armour of the grave with the vestiges of our
    forefathers.

Gwyn Thomas

(Translated by R. Gerallt Jones)

PENMON

To W.J.G.

Fine to remember our jaunt
In high spirits to Penmon.
A marvellous day it was,
Sunday surpassing Sundays;
In this journey we found peace,
Experience of pilgrims.

On Môn, the freshness of May,
On its brim, beauteous Menai's
Filigreed torque stretched like one
Tress of luminous crystal;
Flowers were thick underfoot,
We walked amidst their beauty;
We wished to recall their names
And take two of the fairest
Among them, but could not choose —
Was not each one a jewel?

From bare rock, we heard the cry
Of a gull, salt sea's daughter;
Her wings were beating briskly,
Smooth, bright, like a sword blade's stroke;
She flashed, soared in a spiral,
Turned at the height of the sky;
Sprightly she was and graceful
Lighting on the foam-white crest
Of the wave that danced beneath;
Till lovely was her leaving
Atop the billow's tossings,
Water's butterfly, wave's gem.

And the heron on the verge,
Far off, sea's mournful hermit;
He stood, the blue-grey dreamer,

On a bit of stone, the tide,
Swell's white ferment flinging spray,
Around him playing, rinsing;
He stayed without essaying
A change of look, or one turn,
Listener to the breakers' roar,
Sea miracles' mute watchman.

We reached Penmon and remained
Where summer spread wild roses
On briars like a splendid dawn,
And a blush along the thorn-twigs.

Lovely, once, was the Abbey,
We wondered how it once looked,
And, from the past, before us,
The walls now resumed their form;
Rich craft, its portal and door,
Slender its marble towers;
Haven for the weak its hall,
And holy every chamber;
The dove-cote's turret of stone
Above the berried hillside
Rose to the fair sky's airy
Elation, like sabre or sword;
And there beneath the bushes,
Heavens of leaves for its roof,
The ancient lake sleeps calmly
Below the laced branches' dusk.

At the brink was a cold spring,
And mirror-like its brightness;
As fine as a drink of wine
Its cold foam for a pilgrim.

And then there came a sweet song,
For a brief while, soft vespers;
Concord of bells and organ,
Fleeting voices pouring chant
To heaven's land, in Latin;

Though we searched the scene again,
Nothing more, except the fair
Leaves on the ruin's fragments,
And a deep benign stillness —
Of Môn's monks, we saw no more!

T. Gwynn Jones

(Translated by Joseph P. Clancy)

LLANGEFNI MARKET

1. *The Bull*

a black bull of enormous power
stands in its solitary pen
an inconceivable quantity of muscle
governs its mass.
it makes a bass, husky groan of sympathy
to a beef-cow in a nearby crowded enclosure,
throaty and demoralised, at the second attempt.
its strong, gentle face: the black curls
of a solid Grecian deity.
the eyes of danger and deep water.
the mesmeric stillness, slow blinking.
we wonder at its marvellous career,
the balls slung low like footballs;
small townspeople shaken
by the industry of the carnivores, ourselves.
the rolling eyes of the smell of death.

a farmer passes, on first name terms with the bull.
it ignores him. he criticises the shortness of its legs.
I say, 'They've got a lot to carry', feeling ignorant.
'they won't have after today', he says with
                                        satisfaction.
and we walk away, to the next pen.

2. *The Café*

there are many great wellingtons in the café today,
a masculine air among the housewives.
a stockman sits beside us with a shy grin,
almost a sheep's mouth twist, full of teeth.
blue eyes not right indoors, meant for wind.
he stares ahead, gripping his teacup

in his thumb, saying 'oh aye':
he twinkles into the middle distance.

a year ago today, it was all finished:
they fought the import of Irish cattle
when they could only give their own away
for the meaning of glut is disaster for them.
the farmer gets three times that price for beef now.
they changed the rules because of the song and dance.
'Oh aye, it's very good now', he nods
and swallows his tea to return to the market's rich smell.

Steve Griffiths

PORTH CWYFAN

June, but the morning's cold, the wind
Bluffing occasional rain. I am clear
What brings me here across the stone
Spit to the island, but not what I shall find
When the dried fribbles of seaweed
Are passed, the black worked into the sandgrains
By the tide's mouthing. I can call nothing my own.

A closed-in, comfortless bay, the branchy
Shifts of voyage everywhere. On a slope
Of sand reaching up to the hidden
Field or stretch of marram a tipwhite, paunchy
Terrier sits pat on his marker, yapping me
Bodily out of range. What in God's name is he
Guarding that he thinks I want of a sudden?

To the left is the island, granite-hulled
Against froth, the chapel's roof acute
As Cwyfan put it when the finer
Passions ruled, convergent answers belled
Wetherlike towards God. Ahead is the cliff
Eaten by sand. On the quaking field beyond
Low huts, ordered and menacing. Porth China.

Once on the island those last shingle
Feet I came by seem in threat.
Can you, like Beuno, knit me back severed
Heads, Cwyfan, bond men to single
Living? Your nave has a few wild settles
And phantasmagoric dust. And Roger Parry,
Agent to Owen Bold, has a stone skew-whiff in the yar

Doubling back again is a small
Inevitable tragedy, the umpteenth
In a sinuous month. Now I avoid

The violent pitch of the dog, with all
And nothing to guard, remark his croup,
The hysteric note in the bark. Two dunlin,
Huffing on long legs, pick in and out of the tide.

A man on the beach, a woman
And child with a red woollen cap,
Hummock and stop within earshot,
Eyeing my blundering walk. 'Can
We get to the island?', he asks, Lancashire
Accent humble, dark curls broad. And I
Am suddenly angry. But how is my tripright sounder,
Save that I know Roger Parry and he does not?

Roland Mathias

LLANTYSILIO OVERGROWN

Under the rush of caravans on the Holyhead road
and the thwack in the wind
of the campers' polythene streaming
and the hum of the scale-model traffic
on the miraculous bridges with realistic water below,
the island of Silio hugs its cemetery to itself.

The graves are decked individually
as if each decomposition had its flower:
on dark slate, violet; the spindrift of the disappointed
lips cast from the cheekbone; and these delicate
heavenly ones, nodding at the mild Sunday air
after a lifetime stamped in the gasping furrow.

A green-armed bramble
lances the wind on a thousand tiny fronts
for the unremembered improvisor of hovels,
for tillers and singers, the little stone-skimmers:
a voice secreted over the mouths stained
with their own juices in their made beds.

Steve Griffiths

CAERNARFON, 2 JULY 1969

Castle to castle —
Is there peace?

Those who came for a song
In Lloyd George's parlour
And for a hooray on the field have gone.

The cheer and the boo have gone,
And the proper hats of all the Prince's aunts,
Everyone who said 'lovely', 'love', and 'thanks',
The velvet cushions have gone:
Five guineas' worth of memories.

The policemen have gone,
And Scotland Yard's fill of suspicious names
And pictures and fingerprints.
The cameras and the microphones have gone,
And the cavalry and battalion of dragons
And the clamour about American tourists
And the cost of the plainclothesmen's Bed and Breakfast
And all the rush for the special stamps
Gone.

On the quay, the soldier has gone
In a fiery chariot like some chapter from the Old
        Testament,
And the cry of Llywelyn has gone
And of Owain Glyndŵr and status and 1282.

The sober dignified benches
Have become a hundred thousand planks,
What they were before yesterday and long days before.

Another Prince has started on his journey:

Castle to castle:
Is there peace?

T. Glynne Davies

(Translated by Joseph P. Clancy)

FIRES ON LLŶN

At sunset we climb Uwchmynydd
to a land's end
where R.S. Thomas walks, finding
the footprint of God
warm in the shoe of the hare.

Words shape-shift to wind, a flight
of oystercatchers,
whinchat on a bush, two cormorants
fast-dipping wings
in a brilliant sea.

Over the holy sound Enlli
is dark in a ruff
of foam. Any pebble or shell
might be the knuckle-bone
or vertebra of a saint.

Three English boys throw stones.
Choughs sound alarm.
Sea-birds rise and twenty thousand saints
finger the shingle
to the sea's intonation.

Facing west, we've talked for hours
of our history,
thinking of Ireland and the hurt
cities,
gunshot on lonely farms,

praised unsectarian saints,
Enlli open
to the broken rosary
of their coracles,
praying in Latin and Welsh.

Done with cliff-talking we turn
inland, thinking
of home silently filling
with shadows, the hearth
quiet for the struck match,

our bed spread with clean sheets.
Our eyes are tired
with sun-gazing. Suddenly
we shout — the farms burn.
Through binoculars we see

distant windows curtained with flame.
The fires are real
that minute while we gasp, begin
to run, then realise
windows catch, not fire but

the setting sun. We are struck still
without a word
in any language. See the hares run,
windows darken.

Gillian Clarke

ABERDARON

When I am old and honoured,
   With silver in my purse,
All criticism over,
   All men singing my praise,
I will purchase a lonely cottage
   With nothing facing its door
But the cliffs of Aberdaron
   And the wild waves on the shore.

When I am old and honoured,
   And my blood is running chill,
And watching the moon rising
   Stirs in my heart no thrill,
Hope will be mine thereafter
   In a cottage with its door
To the cliffs of Aberdaron
   And the wild waves on the shore.

When I am old and honoured
   Beyond all scorn and acclaim,
And my song goes by the rubric
   And gone is its passion's flame,
Hope will be mine thereafter
   In a cottage with its door
To the cliffs of Aberdaron
   And the wild waves on the shore.

For there I will discover
   In the stormy wind and its cry
Echoes of the old rebellion
   My soul knew in days gone by.
And I will sing with the old passion

While gazing through the door
At the cliffs of Aberdaron
And the wild waves on the shore.

Cynan

(Translated by Joseph P. Clancy)

WELSH INCIDENT

'But that was nothing to what things came out
From the sea-caves of Criccieth yonder.'
'What were they? Mermaids? dragons? ghosts?'
'Nothing at all of any things like that.'
'What were they then?'

          'All sorts of queer things,
Things never seen or heard or written about,
Very strange, un-Welsh, utterly peculiar
Things. Oh, solid enough they seemed to touch,
Had anyone dared it. Marvellous creation,
All various shapes and sizes, and no sizes,
All new, each perfectly unlike his neighbour,
Though all came moving out slowly together.'
'Describe just one of them.'

          'I am unable.'
'What were their colours?'

          'Mostly nameless colours,
Colours you'd like to see; but one was puce
Or perhaps more like crimson, but not purplish.
Some had no colour.'

          'Tell me, had they legs?'
'Not a leg nor a foot among them that I saw.'
'But did these things come out in any order?
What o'clock was it? What was the day of the week?
Who else was present? How was the weather?'
'I was coming to that. It was half-past three
on Easter Tuesday last. The sun was shining.
The Harlech Silver Band played *Marchog Iesu*
On thirty-seven shimmering instruments,
Collecting for Caernarvon's (Fever) Hospital Fund.
The populations of Pwllheli, Criccieth,
Portmadoc, Borth, Tremadoc, Penrhyndeudraeth,
Were all assembled. Criccieth's mayor addressed them
First in good Welsh and then in fluent English,
Twisting his fingers in his chain of office,

Welcoming the things. They came out on the sand,
Not keeping time to the band, moving seaward
Silently at a snail's pace. But at last
The most odd, indescribable thing of all,
Which hardly one man there could see for wonder,
Did something recognizably a something.'
'Well, what?'
                    'It made a noise.'
                                        'A frightening noise?'
'No, no.'
                    'A musical noise? A noise of scuffling?'
'No, but a very loud, respectable noise —
Like groaning to oneself on Sunday morning
In Chapel, close before the second psalm.'
'What did the mayor do?'
                                   'I was coming to that.'

Robert Graves

NANT GWRTHEYRN

Perched on a grassy ledge,
like some rare sea-birds we feel;
learning the language of an endangered species.

And whatever the reasons that brought us,
the sea shelves at the edge
of our thoughts and the mountains
mouse our trivialities. Shaggy, purple head
of the lying yet waiting peninsula.

The wind's descant and harp-curves
of branches, together in penillion.
Candles are toadstools turned into a rage
of horses by Gwydion's flames.
I am dumb: my mind full of knelling
calls of quarrymen, pulled by the waves' ropes.

Wild goats tread the cliff-path
between reality and myth.
Shy and wary behind a twmp:
hear their night-time rock-fall
as they move in to graze
on pastures which pit beyond our step.

I watch the gradual renovation:
my learning tractored across rough ground
and voice beginning to fit the rhythm
of the carpenter as I feel
around and around, the eddying of Yr Iaith.

See, the granite lies in piles of nuggets
where no boat will beach.
High up to the mountain-top
the stone-supports hoist only cloud.

Listen how we talk and how the sea
rolls boulders from its tongue.

Mike Jenkins

SUMMER IN THE VILLAGE

Now, you can see
where the widows live:
nettles grow tall and thistles seed
round old machinery.
Hayfields smooth under the scythe
simmer with tussocks;
the hedges begin to go,
and the bracken floods in.

Where the young folk have stayed on
gaudy crops of caravans
and tents erupt in the roadside fields;
Shell Gifts, Crab Sandwiches, To Let,
the signs solicit by the gates, left open
where the milk churns used to stand;
and the cash trickles in.

'For Sale' goes up again
on farms the townies bought with good intentions
and a copy of The Whole Earth Guide;
Samantha, Dominic and Willow play
among the geese and goats while parents in the pub
complain about Welsh education and the dole.
And a new asperity creeps in.

Now, you will see
the tidy management of second homes:
slightly startled, old skin stretched,
the cottages are made convenient.
There are boats with seats;
dogs with the work bred out of them
sit listlessly by garden chairs on Kodakcolour lawns;
and all that was community seeps out.

Christine Evans

PART TIMER

Yes, he says, he has
A few pots out from Porth.
Does not explain how from the earliest days
Out fishing with his father and an uncle
It was a refuge from the day's repeated toil:
A different dimension.

    For one thing, no women,
With their nagging at his conscience, or his senses.
Only exhilaration and the early morning air
Rinsing the closeness of the cowpen from his clothes,
Stirring old sediment
Beneath the bother in his brain.

    Now, like a drug,
It draws him more and more.
His eyes are always out beyond the islands,
Sharpening their blue with distance.
He leaves his cows hock-deep in dung
And lets the barley stand;
Fends off his wife to creep out in the dawn
And lingers on the beach
To come home with the tide.

    The lobster cash
Is handy, he will say;
The visitors are always asking for a crab.
And — with diffidence — I don't mind
Going out, I like the fishing all right, too.

                              Christine Evans

115

A WISH

Strange to be seeing waves of the sea
    Like dogs snarling around
Tooth to tooth with the rock, yet we
    Never to hear a sound,
But seeing them, as might
A deaf man's sharp sight.

And strange to listen at night for the cry
    Of some invisible host
When there may be wild geese in the sky
    Across the sounding coast,
And to listen them, the way
The blind listen the day.

If life would give me choice of a skill
    To practise till the grave,
I'd choose to know how to reap my fill
    Of two fields joyous and brave —
Glean them for all they find,
The wise deaf, and the blind.

R. Williams Parry

(Translated by Tony Conran)

BANGOR PIER

(For Luned)

Do you remember the heron
We saw that morning
Poised on the rocks; the thrush bearing
A snail shell, like a death's head warning?

The long strolls on the broken pier
And the wind spying
About our legs with gusty leer,
Smelling of salt; the sea-weed drying

On the rusty ladders and bars;
Tea tuppence cheaper,
But no stronger. There went the cars
On Beaumaris road; the pier keeper,

Like a revolutionary,
Was always knitting,
And we, never in a hurry
For all our work, were always sitting,

Talking, there in the old, cold hut,
And getting nowhere,
Like the boat we watched, that would cut
Back from the steps, into the shattered air.

Sally Roberts Jones

RHYL SANDS

your vision swept clear and bright by the wind that's
                               wiping away the stormclouds
beach low and empty   pale blue sky   seagulls and one dog
                                 near the horizon
pebbles underfoot as clear as the wallpaper in seaside cafés
somewhere out at sea, a rainbow
the sad peeling offseason colours of arcades and kiosks
David Cox's 'Rhyl Sands' a tiny gem burning quietly in dirty
                                 Manchester
ghostly echoes of last season's chip-papers in the drifting sand

      water foaming and fizzing round your warm body
      sudden rush upwards green light everywhere
      sharp salty taste in your mouth your nose stinging
      down again gasping your breath in
      sounds rushing in cries of bathers distant children
      the promenade the Pavilion bright like a postcard

Adrian Henri

SUNNY PRESTATYN

Each day I see them carefully grow old and feed
    behind that glass, those plants,
in an aquarium's stillness — saw at first their need
    for aloneness like a niche.
It is not a need. Lured by sun-crossed memories
    of August, most have retired
from industrial towns at last to find the sea
    sucked out of reach.

They have left the wet streets that flow
    on northern towns like tides,
those separately secret worlds that tow
    forever in their wake
lives bound by the going and returning they inhabit,
    for this quiet place
where silent mornings on the daylight hours sit.
    Here no tide will break.

Some watch the sand, the blank sea stretching out, going
    endlessly nowhere.
Past bungalows, an empty paper bag goes yachting
    down the empty street.
Cars pass; seagulls stream on white safaris to the sea.
    Like their bungalows,
the old here are detached, with no shared memory
    to sift or curse or greet.

And if they had known of this, would they have stayed
    where home and friends
still were, where the family was once, and made
    the most of their discharge?
Anywhere, lack of interest, change and age itself condemn
    them, left on some beach
or trapped in tanks. We are accused of them
    and they are us writ large.

John Davies

STANDING UP

And here's to you in the seaside towns
I've known at the frayed ends of their day:
shining at dusk, you made-up small
hotels about to climb deliberately down
your own steps, and poised there, all

in velveteen and lace after mock-discreet
bar tastings in loungettes where snowy scenes
met plants like octupi. Content, you chose
white plates that showed — under veg and meat,
pulsing through gravy — a lungpink rose.

You turned your backs on those looming
white hotels like icebergs at the reaches
of long drives. What if thoroughbred cars
munched on the gravel there, and booming
bald heads shone? Not for you such stars.

For you all, it seemed, too rapt to be impressed,
they weren't there. You kept your records
and towels clean, chased staff, forgot Who's Who
and advertised. You stood up for second best
(yes, cheers!) as almost all of us should do.

John Davies

GŴR Y RHOS

There is no such thing as the image of a country
For this reason put up this flag for approval:
It is made of skin and stained with sunlight and tobacco
It speaks in pickled phrases the language of apples
And it is wide enough for a shroud.

It remembers the road as a track, pigs
In every sty, a railway running, a harbour
With ships, a quarry working, fresh fish, young people
And planting trees in holes big enough
To bury a horse.

This man is a king except
He makes his living emptying caravan bins
And uses English in the shop to avoid giving offence
To visitors who do not know
Where they are or who he is.

Emyr Humphreys

HOLYWELL

Trapped by the strong favourite of a king,
even Winifred could not deny his sword.
Where hair leaked blood, a well of healing
sprang then the stream's hurrying its hoard
of news woke up the valley. Winifred
drew pilgrims limping, eager to be whole.
He signed up slaves of cotton, copper, lead.
Her stream, severed by water wheels, rolled
machines. When Winifred spread her arms wide
to make from shadows trees, he cut them down
but she thinned the Dee channel — its quayside
became silent, the valley a ghost town.
Now buildings sprawl headless. All around,
sprung green: healing, still misshapen ground.

*

Not just the church preferred its blessings high.
This cotton mill snatched six storeys of sky
with stone from the abbey's broken shell —
then, power overflowing, St Winifred's Well.
An act of God, a world in seventy days.
High too squire Pennant's recorded praise:
the workers flourished, dined on meat and fish
'in commodious houses'. Work was sweet.

Poet Jones of Llansa, muffled voice
of the backwater — why couldn't he rejoice?
'Rods doom'd to bruise in barb'rous dens of noise
the tender forms of orphan girls and boys.'
Poets. They build nothing. Just hover, stare,
write maudlin history. Except he'd worked there.

*

Ingenuity flowers in such fumes.
Copper bolts were roots helping great ships
spread wide. Brass beakers moistening the lips
of Africa, exchanged for slaves, seemed blooms.

Up there, look, a fly-wheel gouged the wall.
In this bank too an opening faced with brick
like an oven drowsily gone rustic;
no grass, webs, wormcasts though. Earth, that's all

almost. Hereabouts being where the knack
of refining human brushes took hold —
twigs bound in rags who carefully swept back
arsenic from this flue and lived to rot —
last year they found a skull, some ten-year-old
ingenuity planted then forgot.

★

The wall here keeps haemorraging dark green
through bricked-up centuries, through soil
Meadow Mill injected with copper spoil.
And its damp spillway's coloured gangrene
in memory of times, as Pennant said,
when workers obeyed 'the antient law'
of sluicing thoroughly before meals or
watched 'eruptions of a green colour' spread.
(Dogs, they knew, if they licked the sheeting slept
for good.) So justice as well, urbane,
copper-bottomed is remembered here. Yet
though the wall's washed scrupulously by rain,
strange that metal still heaves through. Dogs drop.
It has tasted men and starves and cannot stop.

★

Ice tore a trench to the estuary.
Grass healed its sides. Water devised a well.
An idea, grown around it like a tree,
surviving as an arched spell,
towers so pilgrims are beckoned here
still, a welling of belief that named a town.
When another idea for water
bricked up the flow, its weight wore people down.

The centuries keep waking to change dreams.
Dug from undergrowth: brickwork's feud
with stone for possession of the stream.

And voices insisting water is alive —
those pursuing always and, pursued,
some in need of miracles to survive.

John Davies

PIED BEAUTY

Glory be to God for dappled things —
   For skies of couple-colour as a brinded cow;
     For rose-moles all in stipple upon trout that swim;
Fresh-firecoal chestnut falls; finches' wings;
    Landscape plotted and pieced — fold, fallow, and plough;
     And all trades, their gear and tackle and trim.

All things counter, original and spare, strange;
   Whatever is fickle, freckled (who knows how?)
    With swift, slow; sweet, sour; adazzle, dim;
He fathers-forth whose beauty is past change;
               Praise him.

Gerard Manley Hopkins

IN THE VALLEY OF THE ELWY

I remember a house where all were good
   To me, God knows, deserving no such thing:
   Comforting smell breathed at very entering,
Fetched fresh, as I suppose, off some sweet wood.
That cordial air made those kind people a hood
   All over, as a bevy of eggs the mothering wing
   Will, or mild nights the new morsels of Spring:
Why, it seemed of course; seemed of right it should.

Lovely the woods, waters, meadows, combes, vales,
All the air things wear that build this world of Wales;
   Only the inmate does not correspond:
God, lover of souls, swaying considerate scales,
Complete thy creature dear O where it fails,
   Being mighty a master, being a father and fond.

Gerard Manley Hopkins

NIGHTFALL

Silence brought by the dark night: Eryri's
  Mountains veiled by mist:
  The sun in the bed of brine,
  The moon silvering the water.

Gwallter Mechain

(Translated by Tony Conran)

Biographical Notes

PERCY BYSSHE SHELLEY (1792–1822): Romantic poet. Author of a vast body of work. Born in Sussex, he attempted for a brief period to set up a radical commune of 'like spirits' at Tremadoc.

GILLIAN CLARKE: b.1937 in Cardiff. Now lives near Llandysul in Dyfed. Her *Selected Poems* is published by Carcanet (1985).

T. ROWLAND HUGHES (1903–1949): Born at Llanberis, but also lived in London and Cardiff. Best known as a novelist, he also wrote poems, plays and stories whilst suffering from multiple sclerosis.

ROBERT SOUTHEY (1774–1843): Lakeland poet and Poet Laureate, born in Bristol. Author of 'The Battle of Blenheim' and 'The Holly Tree'.

WILLIAM WORDSWORTH (1770–1850): 'Climbing Snowdon' is from his autobiographical verse epic *The Prelude*. Poet Laureate and author of the central Romantic text *The Lyrical Ballads* (1798).

JOHN STUART WILLIAMS: b.1920 in Mountain Ash. Poet and critic. His collection *Dic Penderyn* won him an Arts Council prize in 1971.

T.H.PARRY-WILLIAMS (1887–1975): Emminent twentieth century poet and scholar in Welsh. Born at Rhydd-Ddu in Gwynedd, he was Professor of Welsh at Aberystwyth for some 32 years.

JOHN LATHAM: A Professor of Physics at Manchester. His book *Unpacking Mr Jones* is published by Peterloo Poets.

GEOFFREY FABER: A member of the family behind Faber & Faber, the publishers.

ROBERT GRAVES (1895–1986): First known as a poet of the First World War, and his book telling of his war experiences *Goodbye to All That* was published in 1929. He was a regular visitor to Snowdonia.

RAYMOND GARLICK: b.1926. An Englishman educated at UCNW Bangor who taught for many years in Wales, some of them in Blaenau Ffestiniog. A convert to Wales and the Welsh language. His *Collected Poems* is published by Gwasg Gomer (1987).

HARRI WEBB: b.1920. Bilingual poet, journalist, scriptwriter, public speaker and pamphleteer, his work is described (by himself) as "unrepently nationalistic".

MICHAEL BURN: His 'Welsh Love Letter' is taken from his book *Open Day and Night*.

DUNCAN BUSH: b.1946 in Cardiff. A prize-winning poet, his latest book collection *The Genre of Silence* is set in the Soviet Union during the Stalin years.

BRYAN ASPDEN: b.1933 in Blackburn, Lancs., but lives now in Conwy, having learned Welsh. His latest collection is *Blind Man's Meal* (Seren, 1988).

BOBI JONES: b.1929 in Cardiff into an English-speaking home. By far the most prolific Welsh language writer of the latter half of the twentieth century. Poet, short story writer, novelist, critic and scholar.

A.G.PRYS-JONES (1888–1986): Often regarded as the first Anglo-Welsh poet of the twentieth century. The Welsh nation was consistently a source of pride and inspiration for his work.

JOHN TRIPP (1927–1986): Born in Bargoed, he worked in London and Cardiff. An influential poet much concerned with Welsh nationalism and history. His *Selected Poems* is published by Seren (1989).

HYWEL AB OWAIN GWYNEDD (d.1170): Poet and prince noted for his love poems and his praise of the Gwynedd landscape. He was killed in battle fighting for the Gwynedd inheritance.

GWYN THOMAS: b.1936 at Tanygrisiau and raised in Blaenau Ffestiniog. Poet and scholar, he is now Professor of Welsh at Bangor. Notable for his use of colloquial Welsh in his poetry and his responses to the modern world.

EIFION WYN (ps. Eliseus Williams, 1867–1926): Poet and hymn writer born at Porthmadog. Lived for many years at Pentrefoelas where he was an accountant for the North Wales Slate Company, and a teacher, despite little formal education.

SALLY ROBERTS JONES: b.1935 in London of a Welsh father. She now lives in Port Talbot where she runs Alun Books. Her latest collection is *Relative Values* (Poetry Wales Press, 1985).

PETER FINCH: b.1947. One of Wales' foremost experimental poets. His *Selected Poems* was published by Poetry Wales Press in 1986.

EUROS BOWEN (1904–1988): Although born in Treorchy, he lived much of his life in Bala and Wrexham as a parish priest. Author of fourteen volumes of poetry, he also translated from the Greek, Latin and French into Welsh.

GERARD MANLEY HOPKINS (1844–1889): English poet and Jesuit priest. He lived in Wales for some years and learned Welsh. His poetry was much influenced by the rules of *cynghanedd*. A major influence on the Modernist poets such as Dylan Thomas and W.H.Auden.

THOMAS RICHARDS (1883–1958): Born at Trawsfynydd and farmed at Llanfrothen after spending some time in America. Particularly noted for his englynion of which this is his most famous.

IAN HUGHES: b.1947 in Bethesda. A lecturer at the Normal College in Bangor.

T.GLYNNE DAVIES (1926–1988): Born at Llanrwst, he became a journalist in both languages and a radio producer for the BBC. Author of two books of poetry, two novels and a volume of short stories (Barddas).

FREDERIC VANSON: author of *Spring at Llyn Ogwen* (Gomer) from which this poem is taken.

DAFYDD AP GWILYM (fl.1320–1370): Best known of the medieval Welsh poets, possibly the greatest in the language. He introduced new language, subject matter and techniques to Welsh, including elements of European Courtly Love.

SIÔN PHYLIP (c.1543–1620): A member of a family of poets from the Ardudwy area which tried to maintain traditional, social aspects of Welsh poetry. His work mirrors changes in Welsh society at that time, displaying the new, Elizabethan learning.

WILLIAM JONES (1896–1961): Born at Trefriw. He became a Calvinistic Methodist minister, but left to work as a librarian at Tremadog

BRENDA CHAMBERLAIN (1912–1971): Writer and artist, born in Bangor. Her best-known work is *Tide-Race* (Seren, 1987), and her paintings are in collections worldwide.

CHRISTINE EVANS: b.1943 in Yorkshire. An English teacher who lives on the Llŷn Peninsula. Her third collection of poems *Cometary Phases* is published by Seren (1989).

DAFYDD BENFRAS (fl.1230–1260): A court poet associated with Llywelyn Fawr and Llywelyn ap Gruffyd. A soldier as well as a poet, he died in battle fighting for the then dominant House of Gwynedd.

GWYN WILLIAMS: b.1904 in Port Talbot. Poet and translator. A prolific writer in both Welsh and English, his autobiography *ABC of (D)GW* was published in 1981.

PETER GRUFFYDD: b.1935 in Liverpool and brought up in north Wales. His collection *The Shivering Seed* was published in 1972.

T. GWYNN JONES (1871–1949): Poet, scholar, translator, novelist, dramatist, critic and journalist. He won the Chair at the National Eisteddfod in 1902.

STEVE GRIFFITHS: b.1949. A welfare rights worker in London who was born at Treaddur Day, Anglesey. His last collection is *Civilised Airs* (Poetry Wales Press, 1984).

ROLAND MATHIAS: b.1915 at Talybont-on-Usk. Poet editor and critic who was one of the founders of *The Anglo-Welsh Review*.

CYNAN (ps. Albert Evans-Jones, 1095–1970): Calvinist Methodist minister born in Pwllheli. Served as a soldier and chaplain in the First World War and was a tutor for many years at Bangor. Archdruid in the early fifties he is remembered for his ballads and lyrics.

MIKE JENKINS: b.1953 in Aberystwyth. Editor of *Poetry Wales*. His latest collection is *Invisible Times* (Poetry Wales Press, 1986).

ROBERT WILLIAMS PARRY (1884–1956): Born near Dyffryn Nantlle, Gwynedd and lived for many years in Bethesda. He wrote only two volumes of poetry. *Yr Haf a Cherddi Eraill* and *Cerddi'r Gaeaf*, but was an influential and important poet.

ADRIAN HENRI: b.1932. One of the three popular Liverpool poets, together with Roger McGough and Brian Pattern.

JOHN DAVIES: b.1944 in Cymmer Afan, Glamorgan, but lives now in Prestatyn. Editor and poet, his collection *The Visitor's Book* (Poetry Wales Press, 1985) won the Alice Hunt Bartlett Prize.

EMYR HUMPHREYS: b.1919 at Prestatyn. Novelist, poet and dramatist, he won the 1958 Hawthornden prize for his novel *A Toy Epic* (Reprinted, Seren, 1989).

GWALLTER MECHAIN (ps. Walter Davies, 1761–1849): Poet, editor and promoter of literary standards through eisteddfodau, he was born at Llanfairfechain, and lived for many years at Manafon.

The Translators

R. GERALLT JONES: b.1934. Born and raised on Llŷn, Jones is a prolific poet, novelist and literary critic in Welsh, also a radio and television producer. His *Poetry of Wales 1930–1970* (Gomer) appeared in 1974 and is the source of the translations in this book.

JOSEPH P. CLANCY: b.1928, American poet and translator. His work includes *The Earliest Welsh Poetry* (1970) and *Twentieth Century Welsh Poetry*

(1982), both published by Gomer.

GWYN WILLIAMS: b. 1904. Poet and translator. His books include *The Rent that's Due to Love* (Gomer, 1950) and *The Burning Tree* (Gomer, 1956).

TONY CONRAN: b.1931. Poet, translator and critic. His *Penguin Book of Welsh Verse* was reissued as *Welsh Verse* (Poetry Wales Press) in 1986, and his latest book of poems, *Blodeuwedd* (Poetry Wales Press, 1988) won a Welsh Arts Council Prize.

HARRI WEBB: b. 1920. Often humorous nationalist poet and scriptwriter, author of the influential poetry books *The Green Desert* (Gomer 1969) and *A Crown for Branwen* (Gomer, 1974).

The Editor

TONY CURTIS was born in 1946 in Carmarthen, but spent some of his childhood in Tenby. He is author of a number of collections of poetry including *Selected Poems* and, most recently, *The Last Candles* (Seren). A senior lecturer at the Polytechnic of Wales, he has also edited several critical books and written on Dannie Abse and the reading of modern poetry.

Acknowledgements

For Gillian Clarke: 'Sailing', 'Clywedog', 'Climnbing Cader Idris', 'Castell y Bere' and 'Fires on Llŷn' all taken from *Selected Poems*, Carcanet, 1985.

For T. Rowland Hughes: the translation of 'Crîb Goch' by R. Gerallt Jones from *Poetry of Wales 1930–1970*, Gomer, 1974. The original poem was also published by Gomer.

For John Stuart Williams: by kind permission of the author and Gomer.

For T.H. Parry-Williams: 'Locality' and 'This One' translated by R. Gerallt Jones in *Poetry of Wales 1930–1970*, Gomer, 1974. 'Conviction' and 'Owl' translated by Joseph P. Clancy in *Twentieth Century Welsh Poems*, Gomer, 1982. 'Llyn y Gadair' translated by Tony Conran in *Welsh Verse*, Poetry Wales Press, 1986; original Welsh poems published by Gomer.

For John Latham: 'She'll Be Coming Round the Mountain' from *Unpacking Mr Jones*, Peterloo Poets.

For Geoffrey Faber: the Esate of Geoffrey Faber.

For Robert Graves: the Estate of Robert Graves.

For Raymond Garlick: 'Directions for Visitors'from *Collected Poems*, Gomer, 1988. 'Yours of the 29th' from *A Sense of Time*, Gomer, 1972.

For Harri Webb: 'Postcard from Llanrwst' from *A Crown for Branwen*, Gomer, 1974. His translation of William Jones's 'Young Fellow from Llŷn' was originally published in the *Oxford Book of Welsh Verse*.

For Michael Burn: 'Welsh Love Letter' is taken from *Open Day and Night* by permission of David Bolt Associates.

For Duncan Bush: 'Quarries at Dinorwic' from *Salt*, Poetry Wales Press, 1985.

For Bryan Aspden: 'Chwarel Bethesda: Peter Prendergast' from *News of the Changes*, Poetry Wales Press, 1984.

For Bobi Jones: 'Castell y Bere' translated by Joseph P. Clancy in *Twentieth Century Welsh Poems*, Gomer, 1982; 'Llyn Tegid' translated by Joseph P. Clancy in *Bobi Jones: Selected Poems*, Christopher Davies, 1987.

For A.G. Prys-Jones: the Estate of A.G. Prys-Jones.

For John Tripp: the Estate of John Tripp. All three poems appear in *Selected Poems*, Seren, 1989.

For Tony Curtis: 'Landscape North Wales', 'Landscape North Wales (Reconsidered)', 'The Flooded Valley', from *Selected Poems*, Poetry Wales Press, 1986.

For Gwyn Thomas: 'Horses', 'Cwmorthin' and 'Bryn Celli Ddu' translated by Joseph P. Clancy in *Twentieth Century Welsh Poems*, Gomer, 1982; 'Crossing a Shore' translated by Tony Conran in *Welsh Verse*, Poetry Wales Press, 1986. Original poems published by Gwasg Gee.

For Sally Roberts Jones: 'Snowdonia National Park', 'Treweryn' and 'Bangor Pier' from *Turning Away*, Gomer, 1969; 'Awen: Parc Lake, Conwy Valley' from *The Forgotten Country*, Gomer, 1977.

For Peter Finch: 'A Welsh Wordscape: 1' from *Selected Poems*, Poetry Wales Press, 1987.

For Euros Bowen: the Estate of Euros Bowen. Translation of 'The Quiet Lake' by Joseph P. Clancy from *Twentieth Century Welsh Poems*, Gomer, 1982; 'When the Wind' translated by R. Gerallt Jones from *Poetry of Wales 1930–170*, Gomer, 1974; 'The Swan' translated by Tony Conran from *Welsh Verse*, Poetry

Wales Press, 1986.
For Ian Hughes: uncollected, reprinted here by kind permission of Ian Hughes.
For T. Glynne Davies: Estate of T. Glynne Davies. 'Sentences while Remembering Hiraethog' translated by R. Gerallt Jones from *Poetry of Wales 1930–1970*, Gomer, 1974; 'Caernarfon, 2 July 1969' translated by Joseph P. Clancy from *Twentieth Century Welsh Poems*, Gomer, 1982.
For Brenda Chamberlain: the Estate of Brenda Chamberlain.
For Christine Evans: by kind permission of Christine Evans. All poems from *Looking Inland*, Poetry Wales Press, 1983.
For Gwyn Williams: 'Driving Down the Mawddach from *Collected Poems*, Gomer, 1987. Translations of 'Ode' and 'Exultation' by Hywel ap Owain Gwynedd from *To Look for a Word*, Gomer, 1976.
For Peter Gruffydd: 'Slate Quay: Felinheli' from *The Shimmering Seed*, Chatto & Windus, 1972.
For T. Gwynn Jones: 'Penmon' translated by Joseph P. Clancy from *Twentieth Century Welsh Poems*, Gomer, 1982. Originally published in Welsh by Hughes and Son. By kind permission of the Estate of T. Gwynn Jones.
For Steve Griffiths: 'Llangefni Market' from *Anglesey Material*, Rex Collings, 1980; 'Llantysilio Overgrown' from *Civilised Airs*, Poetry Wales Press, 1984.
For Roland Mathias: 'Porth Cwyfan' from *Burning Brambles: Selected Poems*, Gomer, 1983.
For Mike Jenkins: 'Nant Gwrtheyrn' from *Invisible Times*, Poetry Wales Press, 1986.
For Adrian Henri: 'Rhyl Sands' from *Autobiography*, Cape, 1980.
For John Davies: 'Sunny Prestatyn' from *At the Edge of Town*, Gomer, 1981; 'Standing Up' from *The Visitor's Book*, Poetry Wales Press, 1985; 'Holywell' appeared in *Poetry Wales*.
For Emyr Humphreys: 'Gŵr y Rhos' from *Ancestor Worship*, Gwasg Gee, 1970.
For Tony Conran: the translations of the following poems are all taken from *Welsh Verse*, Poetry Wales Press, 1986: 'Heather' by Eifion Wyn, 'Sheepdog' by Thomas Richards, 'The Seagull' by Dafydd ap Gwilym, 'From Exile' by Dafydd Benfras, 'A Wish' by R. Williams Parry, 'Nightfall' by Gwallter Mechain.
For Joseph P. Clancy: the translations of 'The Seagull' by Siôn Phylip and 'Aberdaron' by Cynan are taken from *Twentieth Century Welsh Poems*, Gomer, 1982.